THE
HEMMING

- - - - - - - - - - - - - -

RECOGNIZING GOD'S HAND
BEHIND AND BEFORE

- - - - - - - - - - - - - -

MELISSA SETTLES

ISBN 979-8-7773-4834-0

Library of Congress Control Number: 2022901984

Interior & Cover Design by Kiley Walker, Noteworthy Creative Group

DEDICATION

This book is dedicated to my husband, Josh, and our two boys, Connor and Cooper. Through the lens of our journey and experiences, I have tasted freedom and seen the hand of the master seamstress. Josh, you are my favorite pastor, my best friend, partner, and the love of my life. And to my mom, Jeannie, who always worshiped in the mornings! Thank you, mom, for taking me to church, demonstrating a kingdom lifestyle, and always supporting me.

You hem me in behind and before, and you lay your hand upon me (Psalm 139: 5 NIV).

As I write this book, looking from behind and before, I will see the hand of the Lord in my life like never before and this will be my stone memorial.

AUTHOR'S NOTE

The ruminations of this collection began over five years ago. I wrote as I was inspired or heard the voice of the Lord. The Hemming, as I knew this work would be coined, would not be complete until I left my job. This is not to say that I hated my job, but quite the contrary. As a four on the Enneagram, I have a huge propensity towards FOMO (the fear of missing out). As such, I felt this longing to experience ministry all- in. I am not the same person I was in 2016, nor is my writing style. Please hold me loosely to these notions, and keep ever before you that we are all works in progress. Look back and forward on your own life and notice the way the Lord has been hemming you in from behind and before- the subtle or frank ways. My biggest fear in you reading this is that I might appear fake in my own eyes, or worse yours. My prayer is that this book serves as either a succession of testimonies or one very big one, and I am satisfied with either. For one moment in my history, I worked up enough courage to stand on the shoulders of a promise and lingered long enough to take it all in.

PREFACE

I feel as though I am sitting in first class, circling. I am in a holding pattern, waiting for clearance to land. The Lord has me waiting for something. He's got me in the belly of the whale, where I cannot escape. I cannot microwave up a quick answer. The attendant is not going to bring me a ready-made itinerary of what is to come. What if I just need to let God be God? In every other season, I've known what to do, how to get better, how to be clean, how to spruce up and shake this off but not this time. I am having to feel my way through... I cannot emergency land. At every emergency exit, there is a huge angel too. In this holding pattern, He wants dialogue, not my usual monologue and or my martyr soliloquy that I know a little too well. He wants my heart, and I want a non-stop service to His heart. I want to be spit up on the dry land of whatever He has for me. I've gotten restless, assured that there is more and I will make sure my seat-backs and tray tables are in their full upright position and that my seat belt is securely fastened. I am ready to move about in what He has for me, everything and nothing less.

TABLE OF CONTENTS

Chapter 1: My Revolutionary Road 01

Chapter 2 : Under Development 07

Chapter 3 : Shelby Lanes 15

Chapter 4 : Saying Yes to the Call 21

Chapter 5 : 1857 Midland Trail 29

Chapter 6 : Asleep at the Wheel 37

Chapter 7 : Elle 45

Chapter 8 : Your Dream is Safe in the Basket 55

Chapter 9 : Resigning 63

Chapter 10 : Relying on Ravens 75

Chapter 11 : Get on with It 85

Chapter 12 : Sifted as Wheat 89

Works Cited 101

About the Author 102

CHAPTER 1

MY REVOLUTIONARY ROAD

- DECEMBER 2016 -

Looking longingly out into the sum collection of my life where it stands, my window acts as my periscope and frame. If happiness is measured by contentment and conformity, I would rank number one in my class. I see the weathered play set anchored to the backyard, that has been a constant for our boys each year. I see the fence that Josh built and assembled by hand, each slate of each board strategically placed to secure the borders of our lot. Behind the fence is the railroad tracks, where seldom a train ever occupies. The slender, barren trees give way to the bright blue sky, where today not a cloud can be seen. Taking in this scene I've seen a thousand times, a restlessness that has become very normal lately evades my mind and billows like fog around my heart. I could stay right here, continue to look out of the same window, see the same scene, and go on making the same memories. Or, I can do something drastic and wild, or at least, that is the way the idea feels as it goes through the veins of discernment.

I'm not sure why, but whenever the idea of walking by faith really takes on a life of its own, it feels foreign to this satisfied and stationary body. What would happen to our spiritual 401Ks if we actually ventured out? What if we stopped doing day in and day out what we cannot stand to do anymore, and allowed ourselves to form and birth a dream? Doing so might mean that I no longer can look out of the same window, to see the same yard. Would that be okay? Would it be a train-wreck? Would I hate myself if this fails? Would I ever again long for the same view of the same yard, even if it makes my chest tight? When did my understanding and my comfort level trump what has been prophesied over me? What if in the letting go, it really meant an opening up? I don't know friends, I don't know, but I never want to be a sell-out for conformity while trying to teach kingdom principles. If faith is really the substance of things hoped for, and the evidence of things unseen- then I must dismantle the safety on my trigger. Shouldn't our spiritual floors be littered with shells and casings of faith and hope aimed and tried, than a perfectly manicured, yet dead lawn that never allowed the rain of faith to fertilize the soil? What good does a conceal and carry license for faith give me, if I never use it? If I don't know how to use it? Or worse, if I never have a time where I have to be brave enough to rely on the faith that is bolstered to my waist? I've flirted with faith, but I've never really given myself over to the possibility of reckless abandon.

I'm tired of being safe and secure and dry on the boat of life. What if I took Jesus at his word? What if I really walked my life out the way I tell others that I believe? What if I looked at my future, not from a retirement sense, but a revival one? What good does storing up on this earth do for me, if in the meantime, I am numb, uninspired, tired, and coasting? I would rather dive in, and have to be rescued by the life preserver of Jesus than to have never felt what getting my garments soaked feels like. All these thoughts race through my mind, and I ease back into the table chair. All this talk of faith is making me hot under the collar and slightly uncomfortable. The doorbell rings, and I abruptly abandon my thoughts to get the door. Two young gentlemen dressed in white shirts and dark dress pants greet me enthusiastically, while handing me a pamphlet. "Where does your faith stand?" they ask, and I smile and look to the road. At that moment, I stood a little taller knowing in my heart and in my spirit that my view of life where it stands right now is changing, and I knew that this could be one of the last times I answer a doorbell at this house, or look out the window from my kitchen and see the same scene.

Our revolutionary road has to start with faith. Stepping into the call of Jesus in your life will be bumpy and cluttered at times. The decision to leave the train of man's approval and climb aboard the train of truth does not come without cost. To follow Jesus and do so with all of your heart, will cost you everything. The tracks of destiny for you have been laid, they have been stretched out between your current address and eternity. Jesus does not expect you to take your seat for this ride blindfolded and scrabbling. He desires to be your traveling companion and your activities coordinator. Jesus is the conductor, and the rails you will be riding belong to Him, were created by Him, and were ordained by Him. Our lives could continue to be scheduled flights where we try to take Jesus with us, and squeeze Him in our day that was arranged by our bills, our children, and our seemingly more important priorities. Or we can do the impossible, and quit. We could quit playing God, we could quit paying wages, tithes, and interest to mammon, and we could actually trust that the steps of a righteous man are ordered by God.

"Now the Lord is the Spirit, and where the spirit of the Lord is, there is freedom" (2 Corinthians 3:17 NIV).

If you have never taken the Enneagram assessment, you should. And really if you haven't, stop right now and do it! I am a 4- the Romantic Individualist. The mundane, ordinary, and done before lifestyles are my kryptonite. There is a chance in faith that I might step out on my revolutionary road and it will not go the way I had envisioned or calculated. Too often, we have bought a new box to put God in and we purchase said box with our conditions already attached. We are willing to give God the glory and the credit for our faith, so long as it looks just like the picture we create in our minds. Jesus is my certainty, and getting to this understanding has been revolutionary. Jesus is perfect in all His ways, and His thoughts are always higher than mine. The journey has been about seeing the hand of God, behind and before, and how He has been setting the stage and the table with the perfect provision. Revolutionizing the gospel means getting to the simplicity of Jesus, and leaning into the sweetness of trusting Him. To trust Jesus means that I can agree to come along for the ride, even if I do not have an itinerary of every future step.

Sounds like the truth, right? Jesus is in the business of tailoring every decision, every high jump from our current glory to the next, and the valleys in between to our destiny.

"For in this hope we were saved. But hope that is seen is no hope at all. Who hopes for what they already have?" (Romans 8:24 NIV).

What is the direction and the thing that you have longed for in your heart, but have not had the guts to start? How many more confirmations do you need?

CHAPTER 2

UNDER DEVELOPMENT

- NOVEMBER 6, 2018 -

What if your delay has something to do with development? I was watching the Disney classic, Cinderella, with my boys this morning and the Holy Spirit spoke to me as only He can. He said that when Cinderella arrived at the palace, she had something to say and she had a skill set and oozed with integrity. My "not right now" is palace training for the days that I cannot even see coming but that were ordained since the beginning of time. Cinderella could not see it, but she was not always going to be living with an evil stepmother and horrid stepsisters. Cinderella did not know that her steps were being ordered, and that she would eventually be a queen.

It has been two years since my Jerry McQuire mission statement and revolutionary road anthem were written. I wrote this manifesto to mark how I stepped out in faith. Josh and I were sure that we were supposed to sell our home, and buy an old Victorian on main street in our small town and fix it up. Josh and I were in agreement, we both felt like the Lord had spoken to us and told us to move forward. We had no contract on the Victorian, but we had faith and so we put our first home on the market. To make a long story short, we moved out of our house in January to an apartment, thinking we would live there temporarily while we fix up the Victorian. We did not close on our house until April of 2017, and the Victorian fell through. The bank appraised the lot and the house and would not lend us the money, because the house did not appraise for the asking price set by the owner. Josh and I had walked the property, spiritually staking it out with our two boys and our golden retriever, Elle. We used to sneak into the old house and walk through it, dreaming of what we would do in each room. The house had a claw foot tub in the upstairs bathroom, need I say more? I remember going to our old house, giving it a final cleaning and walking out of there sentimental but hopeful of what was to come.

All the while, I was not sleeping. At this time, I had struggled with insomnia since January of 2017. Nothing I thought was going to happen, was happening. We were sure that our house would sell quickly, and it was now April and we still had not closed. I thought I was going to buy the Victorian, the whole reason for selling my former home, and that did not work out. I was in a season of utter disappointment. When you are not sleeping, you are not functioning properly. I was tired, angry, and very resentful. We thought by moving to the apartment we were going to save money, but we were actually still making a house payment for a home we were not living in and a rent payment. Nothing was playing out the way I thought it would have. This season had me toying with a question, that within itself had the power to answer everything or destroy everything in one fail swoop.

What happens when you just want to go back to Egypt? At that moment, I questioned God if he had brought me here to die. Sounds dramatic now, but at the time, I was desperate and at one of the lowest places I have ever been. I feel like I stepped out in faith, trusting what I felt in my heart I heard him whisper, and as a result, was starting to feel like I was wandering in the desert. To me, at the time, going back would be better than where I was. We could have moved back into our old house since it had not sold. In moments like this, there is not a Sunday School answer and it is hard to put on a fake smile at church.

Like a light switch, I heard the Lord say to "consider it pure joy when you face trials of many kinds" (James 1:2 NIV). I had forgotten that Jesus is the person from whom all blessings flow- and he does not need to be persuaded on this. He is a good father, and he only gives good gifts. If I am experiencing something in my life contrary to that, it did not come from him. Me getting angry and frustrated at him is disappointment: it's dis-appointing my affection. I cannot get mad at him for something he did not do, and that is where the problem was. I am disappointed in someone that does not disappoint. Romans 5:5 says "hope does not disappoint" (NIV). Jesus can handle us being mad at him. But when it comes to disappointment, he is not the author of disappointment and therefore I have dis-appointed my affection when I do that.

9

The image we see of Pharaoh is the image of our enemy. Pharaoh knew the power of exhaustion and discouragement and he played those cards well. Exodus 5:6 "you are no longer to supply the straw for making bricks; let them go and gather their own straw. But require them to make the same number of bricks as before. Do not reduce the quota" (NIV). We need to build a case, brick by brick, against the enemy- the accuser of the brethren. Adding straw makes the bricks dry quicker and more promptly fired. The straw not only helps the drying process but it adds stability to the brick. Without the straw, the bricks would break and crumble easily. WE NEED TO FIND OUR STRAW. Pharaoh took the straw back and said they would have to find their own. The bricks of life are not going to decrease because I have a straw shortage. The demand is not going to change for the bricks, but I've got to figure out my straw. And in case we missed it, God does not take shortcuts. He is the perfect driver that saw the sign ahead "left lane closed" and went ahead and got over. He is also the guy that allows rude drivers like me to keep driving in the left lane until the very last second and then lets me over with a smile and a wave...

Exodus 13:17 says that "God did not lead them on the road through the Philistine country, though that was shorter. For God said, 'if they face war, they might change their minds and return to Egypt.'" (NIV).

The word Egypt in its original language means Black Land. What took me forever to understand is that the source of my captivity is my enemy. When I hurl insults at God, I am enslaving myself. I do it. I shackle my heart and my mind when I disengage with God and start engaging the enemy through agreement with his lies. Did it ever occur to us that maybe we are not ready to steward the promised land if a little delay and no sleep puts us in this kind of jeopardizing state to just give up? I cannot be handed the responsibility of the deed if I am that easily offended. We are so quick to say we do not want to give the enemy credit, but we never give God enough credit! What I've learned in this season too, is that there are only certain lessons and certain perspectives that can be gained while you're in a valley.

When I was eight months pregnant with Connor, I was leaving school one day and the parking lot was icy and I fell right on my stomach. I was so worried that I hurt my baby when I fell. I got to the doctor, sobbing and snotty, and she assured me that babies in the womb are very well protected, and their mother's body is so well insulated that it is like the baby is wrapped in premium bubble wrap. I smiled out of relief. Those moments and seasons that you are in the valley, you are well protected and armed with premium bubble wrap. The word says "Lord, even when your path takes me through the valley of deepest darkness, fear will never conquer me for you already have" (Psalms 23:4 TPT). What if we loved our Lord back the way He loves us? In another version, this verse says that he makes me lie down. The Lord cannot make me lie down if I am obstinate towards him. Living downtown means that I have to put a leash on our golden retriever, Elle, and physically take her for a walk- a long cry from just opening the sliding glass doors at our old house. Elle will lay down when I ask her to because she trusts me and will obey me and because she is SUBMISSIVE. Maybe reading The Feminine Mystique in college makes me sensitive to submitting, but we must learn that there is a stark difference between loving the Lord and really submitting to His lordship over our lives. When I'm walking Elle and she is fearful, I can barely contain her before she runs scared into oncoming traffic. He is the comforter, and he is with us.

Had I gone back to Egypt, I would have missed what the Lord has for me next. Josh and I finally closed on our first house. I have been sleeping without Ambien since April 5, 2017. We approved house plans and signed a contract with a builder for a new home, and it was finished in December of 2017. Riding the current of disappointment has taught me a thing or two moving forward. Before we settle for going back to a taskmaster and enslaving ourselves, we should learn a thing or two more about the character of our deliverer. I've got to practice wading in the shallows of life to be ready to ride the waves to the deep.

CHAPTER 3

SHELBY LANES

- DECEMBER 16, 2018 -

I grew up in Smithfield, Kentucky, a small town in Henry County. My parents are divorced and my mom remarried my step-dad when I was two years old. My step-dad is Lester, and he was wonderful to me and my older brother, Kenny. If you wanted to do anything growing up, you had to leave Smithfield to do it. We had to go to LaGrange, Shelbyville, or Louisville to shop. One of the things my step-dad enjoyed most was bowling. There was a bowling alley right next to where he worked, called Shelby Lanes. To say I grew up at Shelby Lanes would be an understatement. There were too many evenings to count where I would roam the arcade games while he bowled in various leagues. My step-dad was an amazing bowler. I can just think of those times, and I can hear hundreds of bowling balls hitting wooden pins, cheers of teammates, billows of smoke, the smell of delicious cheeseburgers cooking on a flat top grill, and of course, Atari games for me! I probably played Atari's Pole Position game a hundred times!

When I was around six years old, I remember us all meeting in my living room for a family meeting. My dad told my brother and me that he was considering quitting his job to pursue amateur bowling. Dad went so far as to say that it would mean our family would have to pinch pennies for a while until he got going, but he believed in his dream and wanted to pursue it if we were all in agreement. When I consider what my parents were willing to do in this season for each other, it makes my heart swell. My dad was that good of a bowler, that it just made sense to me at the time. I didn't question their bills, their commitment, man's opinion, dad's retirement, or health insurance. All I knew as a small child was my dad is a bowler and he's pretty good. About a week later, dad injured himself at work. Dad had gotten his hand caught in a machine, and his thumb on his right hand almost had to be amputated. He had to undergo two surgeries and physical therapy for months. His dream of becoming an amateur bowler was finished. With time, he got back into bowling in some leagues. As a child, my parents did not allow this blow to their future to be absorbed by Kenny and me and there was not a lot of talk about him returning to his factory job. I know a dream deferred makes the heart sick, and I can only imagine how grieved he must have been.

Fast forward about ten years, and Shelby Lanes closed down and a new bowling alley, Bluegrass Bowling Center, was opened in Shelbyville. I loved the new building because it was bigger, and more spread out. On the weekends, they turned on the black lights and had more "teenage music," so my friends and I went there often. Dad still bowled in some leagues when the new bowling alley was open. He was a legend there. Everyone knew Lester Waits, his reputation as a bowler, and how big his heart was for people. I remember when I was fifteen or so, my dad took me to the pro shop at the bowling alley and had a custom bowling ball drilled for my right hand. My dad told me that I needed a ball and shoes that were just my size, and that were fitted to my needs. He said no great bowler comes in and uses the same ball and shoes that everyone else does. At that moment, I did not see the need for custom shoes and a bowling ball. I was not a good bowler, I didn't bowl often and I didn't have the heart to tell him no. To this day, I still have that ball, shoes, and even a spiffy case that holds both. I did not recognize the prophetic moment that was happening at that time, but looking back now, I see the hand of the Father hemming all of this together into a pretty special backstory.

- MAY 2005 -

Josh and I were getting married in two months and we were looking for a place to live. He was in bible college in Louisville, Kentucky, and working as a server at a restaurant. I knew he wanted to be a pastor, and I knew my whole life I would marry one. I had finished my undergraduate degree in Secondary English Education, and I had applied to various school districts, eagerly awaiting my first job as a teacher. For us, Shelbyville was the logical place to live because it was central to Louisville and to the church we were attending at the time. Josh and I went to visit a townhome off of Lee's Court, a small street in the Midland Blvd area of Shelbyville. We fell in love with the townhome we saw, and put a deposit down on it and Josh moved in before the wedding. I was living with my parents and stayed with them until our wedding day. Many of our friends questioned why we wanted to live in this "ghetto" part of Shelbyville. To us, it was paradise and a short walk to the gym we went to, and of course, the bowling alley. We lived in that townhome the first two years we were married, and we never had a problem. The area was quiet and it was not until we decided to grow our family that we ever thought about leaving. I look back on those days now and cherish them so much, and the humble beginnings that brought us to where we are today.

_____

_____

_____

_____

_____

_____

_____

_____

_____

_____

_____

_____

_____

_____

_____

_____

_____

_____

_____

_____

_____

_____

_____

_____

CHAPTER 4

SAYING YES TO THE CALL

- APRIL 2010 -

Josh was longing for a ministry position, itching to start doing what he knew he was called to do. I am fretting about the day that I knew would come, where we would leave the church I grew up in, the one Josh proposed to me and we got married in, and the place where I had formed an identity with so many friendships. We were serving and we could have stayed there forever, in what I thought was perfect comfort. The Lord knew my heart needed time; time to accept the change and for my nostalgic heart to prepare itself for the move. I had no capacity to conceive that what the Lord was taking us into was better, and I struggled in letting go of the camp I had set up for so many years.

Josh had accepted an interim youth pastor position at a church in Shelbyville, Kentucky where we lived. Our current church and this new church were great friends, and there were countless services I had attended there growing up. I had been to revival services there that were sparked by a traveling team from Brownsville, Florida in the early 90s. I had seen Jason Upton in concert twice there, and I knew the people there well. For me, leaving my home church was eased in some way by knowing that we were in great hands. We made the transition to the new church in April of 2010, right after Easter Sunday. Connor, our only son at the time, was two and was experiencing some developmental delays. As an educator and a mental health graduate student, I knew something was wrong. My heart and my mind would not allow myself to think he was Autistic.

Josh and I were experiencing an emotionally bumpy road at this point. We watched as Connor's speech deteriorated and we were tired from the constant doctor's appointments that never seemed to go in our favor. We had just entered First Steps, a Kentucky program that comes into your home to evaluate children and follows up with them at their daycare and gives suggestions for therapy. In the midst of all of this, Josh became a youth pastor and we started our journey with a new church family. Looking back on our time at this church, I am so unbelievably grateful for the people that loved us through the hardest season Josh and I have ever faced. By the time Connor was three, he was diagnosed with mild to moderate Autism. I do not think I will ever forget that day when the speech pathologist with First Steps handed me a book and some pamphlets and mouthed those words. But then, God! The Holy Spirit was present in our living room and I had a peace in that moment that surpassed my understanding, that didn't send me into a shame and blame spiral. Up until this point, I had struggled with blaming myself for his diagnosis. I didn't breastfeed, and I sent Connor to daycare at the age of four months where he had ear infection after ear infection. By allowing him to have so many rounds of antibiotics, were we at fault? Am I the worst mom because I went back to work and put my precious, defenseless baby in daycare? Was this because I allowed immunizations? In short, I wanted to blame myself because that was easier than acknowledging the uncertainty. Josh and I immediately started prophesying that Connor is not to be called Autistic, but instead we called him whole, healed, nothing lacking, and nothing missing.

We jumped into speech and occupational therapy three times a week, along with public preschool where Connor now had an Individual Education Plan (IEP). I had sat on the opposite side of the Annual Review Committee (ARC) meetings as the educator and looked on as the parents struggled to hear the progress their children were making, or not making. Now it was my turn to change seats, and be the parent listening to educators tell me what all Connor cannot do. All the while, the church's love and support surrounded us. We were growing in the knowledge of who Jesus really is, and we were casting aside old mindsets that had wrongly attached themselves to us in the process.

A lot of well-meaning Christians will tell you things like "God picked you and Josh to be Connor's parents because he knew you could handle it." My favorite line is "Connor is Autistic because of past sin in your family and this is a generational curse."

One lady offered me some CDs on spiritual warfare. She told me

I needed to get to the generals in the devil's army and cut their heads off to restore Connor's healing. Mind you, at this point in the game, Josh and I were very vulnerable. We are walking this out with our three-year-old son in front of a church body, and I might add here, a very conservative church body. Josh and I were the youngest couple there. Connor struggled with loud music. We might have needed a LeapFrog or other electronic device to keep him occupied. Our glass house was viewable to all and as much as we were trying to trust God, our hearts were broken at watching our sweet boy struggle. I took the CDs from the sweet sister and my plan was to listen to them and ask the Lord what to do with the information. I remember putting the first CD into my car CD player, and immediately the message across the dash screen read "bad disc," and my car spit the disc out. I had never seen that message on the screen before this and I never saw it after. Immediately, I heard the Lord say "I am enough." It was at that moment that I finally understood that Jesus fights my battles for me. He goes before me and sets the table in the presence of my enemies and the battle has already been won. Josh and I spoke truth over Connor daily. We claimed healing and wholeness, and I lived, moved, and had my being in Hebrews chapter eleven. We took him to Cincinnati Children's Hospital for a second opinion. Three separate trips and evaluations later, they told us that Connor was not Autistic but that he did have a developmental delay. Connor was talking, he was reading, and he was doing great. We still had our days and some quirks, but we know that God is the author and finisher of his faith.

Josh and I had been yearning in our hearts for something more, but we were just not sure what that was. God brought Philip and Marsha Clemons into our lives at a pivotal time. Their youth group was flowing in the gifts of the spirit and prophesied regularly. Josh and I finally were experiencing what the more was that we yearned and contended for, but did not have the ability to describe. When you find where you belong, the freedom and the hope that arises is all the confirmation you need. Newfound freedom that is not reciprocated, however, is also quite suffocating. In the months and the year ahead, we were met with more and more restrictions in our current ministry position. When we wanted to do something new or implement anything outside of what was already deemed appropriate, we were told no. It became very evident, though we tried to stuff it down, that the Lord was calling us to something different. Confirmation after confirmation kept coming in from our trusted spiritual parents, from nods and dreams in the night we were both hearing and seeing from God, and we just could not deny anymore what the Lord wanted to do next. When the Lord repeats himself, you need to listen and obey. Josh and I both said many times that it was almost on the verge of disobedience at this point if we didn't follow through.

Some of the best people I have ever met in this life were at our new church. Josh was slated to be the next senior pastor, which included a salary and benefits package. I was working now as a guidance counselor. It is hard to be what you want to be and who you think the church needs you to be when you are divided between your forty-hour work week and ministry on top of that. At this point, Josh was all-in and I was in where I could be and my time would allow. Staying on at this church, as precious as the people were, would have been striving uphill for the rest of our lives. Josh told the current pastor and the elders and deacons that we were resigning, and in February of 2013, we told the congregation. When people asked what we were going to do next, we were honest and told them we had plans to plant a church- something Shelbyville had not experienced or seen before. There were so many prophetic words leading up to this and God was hemming us in, behind and before and he was working the details out before we even knew what to think. What started out frayed and loose, God was hemming into a clear and defined garment of praise and we knew beyond a shadow of a doubt God was about to birth a new ministry.

- APRIL 2013 -

We did not expect to plant The Kingdom House so quickly, but miracle after miracle started happening. Our first location for The Kingdom House was the former Operation Care building on 802 Washington Street, in downtown Shelbyville. The building was so tiny, that we had to turn our pews sideways on an angle just to make them fit. We had one toilet! A random person donated a whole sound system to us, and we were blown away. I just remember being so grateful. When we first started, we held services on Saturday nights. Our family of four were the first members. We had each other, an undeniable word from the Lord, and we set out with no clue, no manual, and faith bigger than Kentucky for what God was going to do. We wanted to be a house where people could encounter Jesus through freedom, hope, and love. Our first service was in April 2013, and people came. Our dear friends, Travis and Shanna Hernandez, whom we grew up with, were coming to help us lead worship on Saturday nights and were still at their current church on Sunday mornings.

We met the Marcums, the Netherys, and many more that made The Kingdom House their home. We believed it couldn't get any better or any sweeter than those times. Looking back, I cherish the early days because we trusted God, we walked by faith, and we were hungry and thirsty for more. While the road since then has had a few bumps, our heart has always been to lean into the Lord's voice and steward the gifts he has given us. Even in a 1,500 square foot building, we wanted to be a sustainable ministry that was not a flash in the pan. We longed to build community, see lives transformed by the love and power of Jesus, and see regional transformation.

CHAPTER 5

1857 MIDLAND TRAIL

- JANUARY 2019 -

Josh and I were about to come up on six years of ministry, and we were busting at the seams of our current church location, 320 Main Street, Shelbyville, Kentucky. We outgrew our first location on Washington Street, and we moved our church to its present location in 2015. Josh and I had just recently joined a CrossFit gym after we met their main trainer, Ryan Oakley. Ryan came to one of our church services and talked a lot about CrossFit, and we were determined to give it a try. We had no idea that the place we came to do our WODs (work-out of the day) and sweat to death, would one day very soon be our second church location. The owners of the gym needed a bigger and more central location. We took one look and knew in our hearts we could renovate this former auto parts warehouse turned CrossFit gym into a church. You should have seen the walls! There were huge cobra snakes painted on them and American flags, and rubber floors for stacks of weights and barbells.

After the new lease was configured, the men in our church went to work and we renovated the space in 30 days! We moved from one toilet to three, and we were on cloud nine. The space was ours and we put some touches to that building that were all us and it was home. The last four years in our current location have been amazing. We have seen God do amazing things, and by His grace and favor, we are still contending for all He has for our community.

Six years in, and Josh is still not full-time, and neither am I. The pace of working full-time jobs away from ministry and trying to be excellent in all you do had begun to take its toll. Josh is a three on the Enneagram, so he accomplishes one thing and immediately moves on to the next, and never slows down to celebrate the victories or to take inventory of the heartbreak. With the growing demands of my job and the needs of a congregation, I found myself feeling like I was not doing anything well. The tension of living in that place where you know you could be doing so much more but you just cannot take on more thing is extremely difficult. Despite our feelings, we kept on and continued to run the race. It became very apparent that we were about to outgrow our second location that had been home for over four years. We contemplated going to two services. Fire code for our space would only allow 100 total people, including children. When everyone is basically a volunteer, and you can barely scrape enough volunteers to cover the nursery as is, going to two services seems impossible. On top of that, our church has such an intimate, family feel, that two services was something I did not want to do just yet. Of the six comrades that comprised our leadership team, we had our two worship leaders, our children's pastor and her husband, who also did our finances and played guitar, and Josh and I.

Shelbyville is a wonderful place to live, but finding a location to house your growing church was a difficult pursuit. We began to pray and started looking for a bigger space. I wrestled with the idea of moving again. Here we are, with approximately one hundred people and the idea of expanding sounds great in theory, but the daily carrying of that is another thing. How were we going to move to a bigger space, with more to take care of, more people, more demands, and no more availability? At the end of the day, Josh is my husband and this impacts our family. People can say what they want, but until you actually walk in the life of leadership, there are a lot of assumptions that we believe and we allow those to encourage us to criticize our leadership. In my mind, this move was not stewardship. How could we possibly steward more? I knew what our days and nights looked like now. When the prospect of the bowling alley first came up, Josh and I dismissed the idea pretty quickly. It would cost upwards of $30,000 to renovate this old space. And even then, we would be renting. As much as we tried, we could not let go of the bowling alley and the prospect of using the space. The business that Josh works for, Andriots, bought the building. Andriots took the first half of the old bowling alley and turned it into their showroom. Kingdom House was given the offer of renovating the back half and renting from Andriots. God's sense of humor is real. We have been waiting for the day when Josh would be full-time. With Andriots buying the building, Josh would literally be at the church everyday of the week. We told our leadership team about our nudge to pursue the bowling alley, they agreed, and we brought the idea to the church. In February 2019, we began the renovation work with hopes to be in by the beginning of August.

- JULY 29, 2019 -

Our first official service at 1857 Midland Trail was July 29, 2019. God was right on time. There was a sweetness in renovating a space that held so much personal and sentimental value to me. God is the best gift giver. He gives us gifts of love that are well thought out and are wrapped in perfect attention to detail. I thought back to the day my dad took me to the pro shop and had a custom bowling ball drilled to fit my hand and my own bowling shoes. I was overwhelmed. Maybe we were in over our heads? Maybe we made a commitment to a space and a budget that was too big or too small? Maybe we don't know what tomorrow holds, but for now, at this moment, all I could feel was gratitude. Some part of me has to hold on to the hope that this is palace training. I have to believe that maybe God is watching how we balance, steward what we have, and give of ourselves in this season. It is heartbreaking to watch Josh not be included in things local pastors get to do during the day because he works a secular job. It is a stretch and a sacrifice for us and our family to pastor a church while we both work other jobs.

In all of the struggle though, there is a sweetness. My God knows our hearts, our desires, and He knows and holds the future. My conventional understanding does not always equate in the kingdom. When did our Instagram stories highlight our reactions to the way the world treats us and makes us feel? As long as I keep responding after the fact and not contending before the fact, my spiritual exercise life will keep circling the mountain. We should always praise and be thankful in all things, but we should also be getting in front of the obstacles and use the Holy Spirit's help to blow a mighty wind of blessing to every circumstance. If I always complain about the outcome of a decision I never take to the feet of Jesus, I have no room to be upset or question His authority. When I command every knee, the knee of my bills, my son's health, the knee of loss and pain, and all knees in between to bow to the name of Jesus, I am thereby releasing the Kingdom to every aspect of my life.

Two church buildings and two renovations made me understand that part of doing good business is leaving a place better than you found it. We did not move into the Victorian and have Chip and Joanna come out and pay their respects to our renovation skills. We did, however, renovate two church buildings and have been used by God to renovate lives. The owners of our second building were so pleased with what we did to that space, that it has forever changed their clientele moving forward. Us occupying that space helped increase the value of the whole building. Now that we are in our current location, the owner of that building tells us all the time how blessed his business is due to God's presence. When you release the kingdom, everyone benefits. Sometimes when I walk into our building for service or worship community practice, I will stand in the parking lot and look back to the townhome we lived in as a newly married couple just a few yards away. God knew this would one day be our home, and I love how he positioned me near it for a custom bowling bowl and shoes, and as a new wife. The dreams God has placed in you to do might not take shape on your timetable, but he is moving. How lovely is God that he took all those experiences that he knew meant something to me, and planted us right in the middle of it?

CHAPTER 6

ASLEEP AT THE WHEEL

- SEPTEMBER 2020 -

The Lord has a sense of humor! In all the times and ways I blamed my job for my unhappiness, Covid-19 came along and made me super thankful for the job I have. I was able to keep working and keep paying my bills and feed my family during one of the craziest times in my history and the world. I interviewed for a position at a different district during the Covid pandemic and decided that now was not the time to be moving districts and possibly being on a different schedule than my sons. When Covid first hit, we were all sent home. What was supposed to be three weeks, turned into the rest of the school year. Being a high school guidance counselor is hard, but doing my job virtually while simultaneously teaching my own children is insanity and the hardest thing I have ever done. There were days that we all cried trying to balance all the things and sharing the wifi for three zoom calls at one time. In the midst of the scary and the hard, I was also grateful. Short of having another maternity leave, I might not ever get that kind of time at home with my kids again. We took walks, we read books, we cooked together, and we appreciated our health and that of our loved ones so much more. If anything positive was coming out of this time, it was the connection families were making with each other again.

When schools closed, the announcement was made by our governor that churches had to close as well. In March of 2020, we started live streaming our services with Facebook Live. Pastoring a church during a global pandemic is not easy, let me tell you. Josh and I were struggling to parent, struggling to balance working from home and teaching our kids. On top of an already difficult situation, we added the layer of ministry. I felt like we were being hit on all sides. You have the one side of the church that is breathing down our neck to stay open, despite what the governor has ordered. We were being accused of having little faith and being fearful of man and not god. Then on the opposite side, we had people upset with us that were not taking more precautions and we were being negligent if we did open our doors. Josh and I felt like we were in the middle of a polarizing divide and no matter what we did, we were going to upset someone in the process of trying to do what we felt was the right thing. I started to question my own judgment. I began to shut down. I was so stressed from my job that I literally could only focus on not having a nervous breakdown. I am a high school guidance counselor and one of the biggest jobs of my year is scheduling. In a normal school year, February to May is a whirlwind and you hold on while the tornado sweeps through. Trying to contact students, obtain their scheduling requests, reach out to my failing seniors, and everything became suffocating and unbearable. I was working during the evenings, nights and weekends just to keep up. Our oldest son is autistic and he needs help with his school work, so I became a surrogate special education teacher. Our youngest was seven at the time and he needed constant support and supervision and NTI became synonymous with hate, bitterness, and sadness. I missed my office. I missed my students. I had taken for granted that during a normal school year I could speak to them, see them, answer their questions, and conduct life so much easier. My poor eyes were like "no ma'am" from the constant screen time and I had to put deep breathing and yoga apps on my phone to survive. So many things in my life were on autopilot. I was running on reserves and those were starting to fail. There is not a manual for how to pastor, and there for sure is not one on how to thrive in a pandemic. When our governor permitted churches to reopen with restrictions, we opened our doors on the first Sunday we could. Half of our congregation expected us to allow them to come in without a mask and congregate and carry on as normal, and the other half were looking at us like "aren't you going to address this behavior?" Josh seemed unfazed and carried on leadership as usual and probably better than ever. I had gotten to the point where I fell asleep at the wheel spiritually. I had no fight, no drive, and I was allowing the opinions of everyone else to determine what I thought. As a public school employee, certain things like masks were not an option or up for spiritual or political opinion. I remember there was a day in August when I just started journaling my thoughts and it went something like this:

There is a tide that has the power to pull us out into deeper waters of fear. The beaches of our decisions are met with so many unknowns and changes, and we are growing even more exhausted in the struggle to understand, much less advocate. Our minds are stifled, our ideas suppressed, and our safety rafts are now needed to carry 100 more. The waves keep coming with no reprieve, and the undercurrent of fear, worry, entitlement, and inconsistency is pulling us out even further with reckless abandon. Capsizing is inevitable. If we do not get to higher ground, and fast, life will squeeze the most out of us.

It amazes me that we have been reduced to being the most comfortable around the people that are the most guarded, the most fearful, and the most careful. We no longer gauge comfort based on relationship, but with how well they follow the rules. The sides have been declared and the battle lines drawn, and you're either with us or you are against us. If you do not think like me, talk like me, post social media posts like me-then unfollow me, and I'm done with you. What we used to respect, we now cannot tolerate. If we do not get to higher ground, and fast, life will squeeze the most out of us.

There are people we metaphorically or literally bled with, endured crazy times with, and who in a former life might have been called our brethren: and are now on the other end of a polarizing divide. Under my mask I'm smiling. Under my mask, I'm struggling. Under my mask, I'm hurting. Under my mask, I'm many things. What keeps me up at night is that we are not getting close enough to notice these things. Not everything can be picked up by video, by zoom, or by 6 foot social distancing. We are saying things to each other we would never say. "That's what you get because you didn't wear a mask." Jesus help us. If we don't get to higher ground, and fast, life will squeeze the most out of us. Life will squeeze our joy if we do not do something. Fear is winning if we do not do something. I am not suggesting this virus is fake or that taking precautions is not smart. What I am suggesting is that there is tide masquerading itself as precaution but is trumping presence. We are so afraid of what we might get that we have sacrificed what we need to get on the altar of exchange. Have we forgotten who we serve? Have we forgotten who is on the throne? The only thing that will drive this tide back and calm the waves is perfect love.

There is no fear in love. But perfect love drives out fear.

What if higher ground looked like less judging? What if higher ground looked like speaking truth in really hard places, but saying it in love? What if higher ground is not condemnation for what someone did, didn't do, or didn't know they were doing? What if higher ground looked more like understanding, respecting that things are so unpredictable and crazy, and shared responsibility? Higher ground looks like grace– grace to the mom who wants to keep her kids at home, grace to the mom that needs to send her kids back, and grace to the mom that forgot her mask when she walks into the store.

Higher ground is realizing that the only thing I can be certain of is how much Jesus loves me. For me, much of this season has been dictated by what the Governor tells me, what the CDC says is permissible, what the school district believes, and I keep asking myself- "what do I believe?" I believe we can turn the tide. I believe that our latter days are going to be better than our former days; that means a shift is coming. I believe what the enemy intended for evil, God is using to rebuild for the good. I believe when we start decreeing and declaring the goodness of God instead of dwelling on the attempts of the enemy- our outlook and our forecast will change. I believe when we start supporting each other and stop assigning sides, we could really unify and take back what the enemy has stolen.

These thoughts turned into prayer and soon I was fully aware of my spiritual condition. I had allowed fear and unworthiness to drive my spiritual car and I had fallen asleep at the wheel. I desperately needed and wanted to wake up. As a pastor of the house, I realized how dangerous sleepwalking is when you are in a leadership position. I had become lukewarm, passive, and my heart was grieved by how far I had fallen. I sought the Lord, cried out to him, and repented for the way I was conducting my life. I could not take another minute of pleasing everyone else, and not pleasing God. I knew in my heart that I needed to say I was sorry to the church. The following Sunday, I did just that. I apologized to our congregation that I had not taken a more active role in leading, that I was not making conscious efforts to partner with the Holy Spirit to see change and for God to move, and expressed my deepest sorrows for my recent slumbering. During worship that day, our team sang "Draw Me Close to You," and I was undone. This was my cradle song. When I was feeling like I needed to be energized and fully present, God was asking me to rest. Hope and rest in the Lord energizes us. My eyes were starting to take their gaze off of man and put them back on Jesus where they belonged. It was in the resting and the holding that my heart was restored and my eyes were opened.

CHAPTER 7

ELLE

- NOVEMBER 9, 2019 -

Our family has a Golden Retriever named Elle, and she was ten and a half. I grew up with a Chihuahua named Buttons, and she lived to be eighteen years old. Buttons was a small and ferocious dog, and she only really loved my parents- she tolerated my brother and me. I will never forget being five and coming home from a weekend at my dad's house and there she was, sitting with my mom in the recliner. As mean as she was, I loved her. She added comedy to when my friends came over, and she had a pesky habit of hiding food in our shoes. Buttons died the week before I got married. I was twenty-three years old when my parents lost our childhood pet, and I watched the grief storm in on them at a time when they should have been the happiest. Having a small dog my whole life made me know that I wanted a big dog that not only loved me but everyone.

When Josh and I were newly married and living in a little apartment, I remember the days when I read John Grogan's, Marley and Me. I loved his story of what a rascal Marley was at first and daydreamed of such a friend. As I read more, my heart broke when the wife lost her baby and Marley stayed with her and had this keen sense that something was wrong. As the story went on, I picked up on the foreshadowing of what was to come for Marley. I remember laying on our couch reading while Josh was studying and I began to cry and I said "Marley is going to die." I had no pet at the time, but the pain and the grief coming off of those pages was palpable. Naturally, I watched the movie too, and what a sob fest it was! It's not like I didn't already know how this was going to end, and I think everyone who gets a pet knows how the story ends.

I knew at that moment I wanted a dog, despite the ending, I wanted one desperately. Josh and I went to a local shelter and began looking for dogs. We found a sweet little mutt and we begged our landlord to say yes. We picked this dog up on a Thursday maybe, and we named her Molly. Molly was used to being in a kennel, and housebreaking was not going to be easy. I had a good weekend with her. When I came home Monday from work, she was not in the house and her crate was gone. Josh had taken her back to the shelter, without asking me or discussing it while I was at work. I could have killed him for taking this dog back without even telling me, but looking back, it was the best thing he could have ever done. The apartment was not a place for a dog and we were not ready. What I really wanted was a baby, and then a dog. That summer, Josh and I purchased our first home. Right after we moved in, I found out I was pregnant with our first son, Connor. Now that we had our own house, a backyard with a fence, we knew it was time to find a puppy.

My whole life, I had dreamed of having a Golden Retriever. We started the search, and went looking for puppies in Louisville, Kentucky. We met the breeder and put down a deposit, left their home, and couldn't shake the feeling that their dogs were not for us. The next day, we made a trip to Meade County, Kentucky because we heard that a local couple had purebred Golden Retriever puppies for sale. We get there, and I see a very petite mother looking over her beautiful pups in this plastic kid's swimming pool. The owners lived in a double wide trailer in the middle of nowhere and all I could see were these cute puppies. The owners told us they were eight weeks old and if we wanted to see the father, he was on the premises too. We walked back to the other side of their house, and there was this huge male golden, whose coat was very red. The owners told us that they didn't know if the puppies would take after their mother or the father, because this was their first litter. Josh said he wanted a lighter colored one. When I got near the pool, this one little girl kept coming to me and I knew then and there I wanted that one. I will never forget us leaving with Elle, she was so small and fit in Josh's lap perfectly. We drove away in our Pontiac Sunfire into the sunset with a golden girl that would change our lives. Connor was one when we got Elle; they grew up together. She was easy to train and was so well behaved. Elle was perfect with Connor and perfectly greeted Cooper the day we brought him home from the hospital. Elle was the most beautiful Golden Retriever I had ever seen, and possibly the nicest. Elle liked donuts so much, that one time she swallowed a full sized rope toy WHOLE in order to get one. I will never forget her standing in our kitchen, tail wagging when I asked her if she wanted a donut. Josh was giving Connor a bath and he had strict rules about not feeding Elle from the table. I thought I could feed this to her quickly and he wouldn't suspect a thing. Elle came right up to me, a rope toy in her mouth, and sat down. I said, "Elle, would you like a donut?" Without even batting an eye, she swallows the rope toy in one gulp and continues wagging her tail and shaking her backside as if to say "anytime now." I eventually told Josh what I had done, and I will never forget the phone conversation with the vet. This happened mid- week and we had a youth conference that weekend that Josh was speaking at and the elders from the church he was about to be hired at were coming to hear him speak. The vet told us that she would either pass it or she would have to get surgery to have it removed. We followed Elle around for the next three days waiting for her to pass that rope. I knew if Elle didn't, her fate was not good- because Josh is frugal and he would not have paid whatever it would have cost me to fix her when it was my fault. The day of the youth retreat, Elle passed the rope toy in its entirety and Josh used her story as sermon material that weekend! Elle was the subject of many sermon illustrations for years to come, and one of my favorite memories of her was when she came to our 320 Main Street location as a live sermon illustration. Josh was preaching on the Holy Spirit and knowing our worth, and taking her leash off and watching her strut around in that church was by far my favorite moment. I'm so glad we did that when we did.

I began to notice that Elle was not eating much, which is not like her. Elle's normal eating habits include almost choking because as soon as it hit the bowl, she was inhaling the food. For a couple of weeks, she went a day or two without eating, and finally I made an appointment to take her to the vet. I was expecting them to tell me she had some kind of bacterial infection and give me some medicine and we would be on our way. The day I took her to the vet was on Saturday, October 19, 2019. The vet assistant said they would run some blood work and do a physical exam. When they took Elle out of the room, she didn't return for about 30 minutes. The vet brought her back in and told me that when he felt her abdomen, something did not feel right. He asked me to follow him back to see some x-rays. Following the doctor back into that room, seeing parts of the vet's office I had not seen before, made the pit of my stomach turn. He showed me a picture of Elle's abdomen and I could see a very large mass that was easy to make out to the naked eye. He told me that her intestines should be occupying that space, but because the tumor was so big, it was pushing her intestines all the way down to the very bottom of her abdominal cavity. He explained that this is why she might not be eating as much. He mentioned something about an ultrasound, but by then I could not hear anything else. All I could see was this x-ray and this room. I could only hear the tone in his voice, the way he didn't make eye contact with me. All I could feel was sadness. She was my person. I was not expecting this news, I was alone with Elle at the vet's office, and I knew at that moment this would be the last time I would bring her to the vet for a well visit. The vet told us we could do exploratory surgery but at her age there was no guarantee. If they opened her up and found that the tumor had grown into and was entangled with her other organs, there would be nothing they could do and they would put her down right then and there. You really do not have the presence of mind to ask important questions at a juncture like this. I picked myself up off the floor and walked back to where Elle was. She knew I knew. Tears were streaming down my face and uncontrollable sobs began to come from a place of helplessness. The vet and the assistant helped us out to the car. Even when she did not feel good, she still smiled and she was still so sweet.

In the next day or two, Josh and I weighed the options. Elle was my classy lady, and she was too regal and royal to be cut open and put through a surgery that may or may not even work. The surgery was going to cost us $1800 just to cut her open and look. My first reaction was to pay it, I would do whatever it took to give her a chance. The longer I thought about it, the more I knew I couldn't do that. We got some solid advice from a different vet that works at the same clinic and he said to take her home and to enjoy her and what time she had left, and that is what we did. For the next three weeks, we soaked up every moment with Elle. We spoiled her with table food, even steak. Elle seemed great, she was eating, playing, and her quality of life was amazing until it wasn't.

On Friday, November 8, 2019, she took a turn. She was not getting up too much and laid around all day. Josh and I started the real conversation of maybe it was time. On Saturday, November 9, 2019, Elle laid down and never got back up. She was not crying or in distress in that way, but knowing her, I knew she was in pain. I think if it was up to her, she would have stayed with us as long as she could. That day, I laid with her on the floor and I seared her face into my memory. I stroked her head and I cried with her. I told her she was the best girl. Elle was laying on the floor in front of our couch and I laid on my left side and my face was right with hers. As a four on the Enneagram, this was both beautiful and the most painful thing I had ever done. Around 9:00 p.m., Josh took her and met the vet to have her put down. I never imagined things would happen this way because I always thought I would be in the room when we put her down. Our boys were at home with us and I could not put them through witnessing this event, so I made the hardest of decisions and helped load her into the back of Josh's Jeep. Watching Elle leave the house alive knowing she would not return that way was heartbreaking. I do not know if we made the right choice, but I know I couldn't watch her deteriorate. Josh brought her body back and wrapped her in blankets in the garage. We had church the following morning, and buried her in the backyard once we got home.

Right after Elle died, I developed an allergy in my left eye that made my contacts unwearable. For two weeks, I could not figure out what was going on in my eye. I went to my eye doctor and was prescribed steroid drops that I repeated for several days and weeks to no avail. It was not until I went to see a friend who does acupuncture that I realized grief and trauma affects the body. I did not want to admit that what happened to Elle was a trauma, probably because I have counseled people with their own traumas. My practitioner told me that my eye saw her die, and my body wants to protect itself from feeling that again, so my body had developed an allergy to the contacts I was wearing while I laid on the floor with her. Sounds crazy, but it was all real and true for me. I needed to allow my body to grieve her passing. I did not realize how much she was a therapy dog to the stressful life I was leading until she was absent. Elle meant so much to me that she earned a chapter in the book where I talk about the goodness of God and how he uses every detail of our lives for his glory. Elle died in November, and in February of 2020, I got Lasik surgery. I was seeing 20/20 in 2020, both naturally and spiritually.

CHAPTER 8

YOUR DREAM IS SAFE IN THE BASKET

- JULY 2020 -

Our family loves to go to the beach every summer. When I am at the beach, I reflect. I think the pace of the week is so slow, that normally things surface that I do not always intend for or plan to encounter. In January, I read a devotional by Bob Goff and had so many confirmations about pursuing ministry full-time, and yet, I found myself at the beach still gainfully employed in the same job. It was at the beach that I realized I would be taking a few weeks off only to return to the place I had planned to leave. Josh had started and finished real estate school during the pandemic. He was just about to launch his real estate career, still pastor the church, and work at Andriots. In my mind, I knew that I needed to stay at my job for another year at least to help stabilize our income and help offset Josh's third job. Even though he assured me this third venture would help be a means to the end of my job, I still did not quite understand. Why are we taking on more jobs when I desperately need to leave mine? Staring into the beach waves,

I started to feel like I had put my dreams in a basket to float down the river. This felt like I was abandoning the desires of my heart, but the Lord showed me that week that what I was doing was not killing my dreams but saving them. What cannot survive in our hands has to be handed over to a loving God who can breathe life into things and put our dreams and destinies into motion.

From here, I started learning about Moses' mother, Jochebed, which means Yahweh is glory. Her story can be found starting in Exodus chapter one. The new king of Egypt was greatly disturbed how the Israelites continued to multiply despite harsh treatment and forced labor. He issued a decree that all baby boys born to Hebrew women were to be killed. When he was not successful at using the midwives to carry out this terrible order, he summoned all the people to throw male babies into the Nile. Jochebed was able to hide Moses for three months. Scripture tells us that "when she could hide him no longer, she got a papyrus basket for him and coated it with tar and pitch. Then she placed the child in it and put it among the reeds along the bank of the Nile" (Exodus 2:3 NIV). The papyrus basket was formed by a mother who knew what she was doing. Egyptian river boats were made with these same reeds and waterproofed with tar. The reeds grew as tall as 16 feet, so she could hide the basket there while she made it. Jochebed did not just throw her baby into the Nile, as the order told her to do. Jochebed made a vessel for her baby to travel in that would keep him safe and secure.

To tar and to pitch means protect, waterproof, or seal. Our heavenly father is not asking you to drown and kill your dreams, but he may be asking you to tar and pitch what you have so that your dreams stay dry, protected, and sealed from attack. I might not be able to have all I want for my dream right now, or provide for it the way I want to- but I can tar and pitch what I have. The dream in my hand will die, but the dream in the hands of a loving savior will live. Moses needed a different environment to not only thrive, but to live. The promises and the dreams of god will come to pass, but it takes an obedient heart with a listening ear to make what could have been a disaster a divine appointment. God did not require any special training from Jochebed to prepare the vessel for her son, but to use what she had and to put to use what she knew. We think the little moments and the time in be- tween is insignificant, but nothing is wasted with him. You and I may not view the inanimate things around us as noteworthy, but God can and will certainly use them. What we think are insignificant details- God uses to form and fashion history and promised lands. Just think of the jobs and the knick-knacks your grandmother and grandfather had! You were not just dropped here, but fashioned. Everything about your life is important and it's valuable to God.

One of my favorite toys to play with at my Mamaw and Papaw's house was an old-fashioned phone they had in their bathroom. Ev- ery time we would visit them, I spent most of my time in their bath- room pretending to make important phone calls with that pretend electric candlestick phone. When my papaw died, all I wanted was that phone. It was not until I was an adult, that I realized that phone was actually an Avon Men's cologne holder. The toy that brought me so much joy was now a relic and a link to the most precious man I ever knew. I unscrewed the top of that cologne holder and breathed in a lifetime of memories and the sweetest fragrance my heart and my emotions could ever handle. God gives us kisses like these all the time, and when He does, I am sure that "the steps of a man are established by the Lord, and he delights in his way" (Psalm 37:23 NIV).

Moses' mother tarred and pitched his basket and placed him on the Nile. What you might be barely floating in right now will one day be the same environment you are placed in authority to lead and to part. I grew up running around a bowling alley, playing arcade games. The same bowling alley is now the place where Josh and I pastor our church! I wrote in diaries as a kid, had notebooks filled with bible study notes from my teenage years, and drove home every Wednesday night and every weekend from college to go to church. My life and the little things I think are insignificant are not small to God. He will use you, and he will use your past to form the present. Moses was made for water. He was drawn from it and eventually led people through it. Moses was delivered in a basket, and he was later used by God to deliver his own people. My mind wonders though, what Jochebed was thinking. My heart goes out to a mother making the hardest decision of her life and the conversations that were not recorded in scripture. I wonder what Jochebed said to her baby? I think about how hard that must have been to take a 3-month-old that you just got in the swing of nursing and put him in a basket you made yourself knowing this was the only way. I imagine she took great pride to make sure that basket was wired for safety, and she must have taken all night to interlace the material and triple check and then check again. I imagine she had some sleepless nights, and worked when baby Moses napped. I think about the tension she must have felt to want to cuddle and hold her baby but the pressure she felt to complete the mission. What was she thinking as she put the basket in the water and pushed him away? I wonder what her other children thought, what did she tell Miriam who was with her? The prayers of our mothers make all the difference. The care, the attention to detail, and the investment into our growth and protection are unmatched.

Jochebed's faith was unparalleled. She knew putting Moses in the water was a risk, but rather than hashing out the what-ifs, she sought the Lord and traded those in for the even ifs. Sometimes we have to put our dreams in a basket to flow downriver and give them to God because if they stayed in our hands, there's no way they could make it or survive. This gesture is not giving up– but giving our dreams over. If Moses' mother had kept him, he would've died by Egyptian hands. So she did the next best thing she could think of. We have to surrender our dreams to see them resurrected. Putting your dreams in a basket to float downriver is abandonment to the heart of God and to the will of God. A seed has to die when it's planted in order to bring life.

"Let me make this clear: A single grain of wheat will never be more than a single grain of wheat unless it drops into the ground and dies. Because then it sprouts and produces a great harvest of wheat- all because one grain died. The person who loves his life and pampers himself will miss true life. But the one who detaches his life from this world and abandons himself to me will find true life and enjoy it forever " (John 12:24-25 TPT).

Putting our dreams in a basket to flow downriver is not an end, it's not a bad thing, but it's a surrender thing. There is more in store for your future than what you are seeing right now. "There's never been the slightest doubt in my mind that the God who started this great work in you would keep at it and bring it to a flourishing finish, to the very day that Christ Jesus appears" (Philippians 1:6 MSG). Nothing is ever wasted with God. What you lay down today, will be used tomorrow and in the future. And it will be used in the coolest way.

God repurposes.

He remodels.

He renovates

He recovers.

He regenerates.

He reduces.

He reuses.

He restores.

He refreshes.

He revives.

He refurbishes.

He rehabilitates.

He remakes.

He revamps.

He renews.

HE RESURRECTS.

CHAPTER 9

RESIGNING

- APRIL 2021 -

The idea of leaving my job as a full-time guidance counselor really started to swish around in my mind over a year and a half ago. I loved working with kids and I absolutely loved the team I spent my days with at school, but my heart was craving something else. I remember a couple of years back, I read the daily devotional Live in Grace Walk in Love by Bob Goff and felt like confirmation greeted me on every page. My job was all-encompassing. On top of that, we were trying to manage ministry and our own kids and I just felt like I was failing at everything. Something was different about this season, though. Josh and I had this dance we did every spring where we talked a good game about me leaving, but I always pushed it down and kept moving in the same direction. For the first time, it really started to seem like it was a possibility that I could resign. In February of 2021, I saw a post made by Eric and Candace Johnson talking about their transition away from Bethel.

I did not see the post until late January or February, but it was posted in December of 2020. In the post, he talks about letting go of certainty and becoming friends with uncertainty. Eric included a quote from his friend, Randall Worley, that sent me on a search for anything of his I could read. The quote he included in the post said "'Our lives are more regimented and routine providing security in the daily sameness. But faith embraces the ambiguity of not knowing where it is being led, because it is so in love with the One who is leading.'" I truly think Eric's post was a timely plumbline for me to really evaluate my life of faith. From this post, I ordered Randall Worley's book, Wandering and Wondering. To say this book changed my life is an understatement. I have never read a book that was so spiritually challenging. I pick up books to read and many times put them down because they just do not have meat and content. Randall crafted a spiritual lightsaber that pierced the dark places of my soul. Every page I read either had me in tears due to the conviction and confirmation, or it had me searching for the meaning of words on my dictionary app. I felt like the Lord was nudging me along a path to trust Him.

On March 23, 2021- I wrote in my journal I feel like I am in this place of indecision. Part of me wants to step out, and part of me knows it's safer to stay. I wish I knew exactly what to do. I knew what I was supposed to do, but knowing it and doing it are two very different things, aren't they?! So often, we know what we need to do. We know what would put fear in a chokehold and yet we allow fear to keep backing us into a corner. For me, it had finally come down to a very simple question: do I trust God or do I bow to fear? I had been eating a steady diet of fear for long enough. Talk was getting cheap, and I knew that if I was going to make this huge decision, I needed to do it soon. It was already April, and I knew that if I was leaving, I needed to tell my principal soon. I already felt like April was late, and I could not put off this decision much longer.

The wrestling that took place in my heart over that month was insane. I came up with every reason you can imagine to stay. One of the biggest pulls to stay was my oldest son, Connor. Connor was in 7th grade at the time, and I knew he would be at the high school I worked at in one year. Part of my decision to become an educator was to be on the same schedule as my kids. If I didn't get into this work to be with them, why did I? Connor is on the spectrum, and routine is huge for him. His whole life had operated under the knowledge that mom was an educator. He grew up in the halls of Collins High School. He came to my work every day after school. I knew that if I stayed long enough for Connor to get to high school, I would stay four more years. Then if I stayed four more years, my youngest would be hitting middle school and it would only be a matter of time before he was in high school too. If I did not get out now, I wouldn't. I write this like it was an easy decision, but that piece of it made my choice very difficult. There will always be a part of me in the years to come that will grieve not having that experience with Connor. But here's the thing; it's either grieve that experience with him or have a heart that is sick from a dream deferred… Either way it hurts.

I was preparing to preach at our church for the April 11, 2021, Sunday service. My heart had been in the book of Exodus for months. I knew Jesus was calling me out of Egypt. Unlike the Israelites, I did not have a Moses. I wonder if the Israelites would have left on their own without Moses? The only person I had to blame for making this decision was myself, and that is no small thing. If I step out and this falls apart or goes well, I live with the consequences of the decision. I did not have a Moses, but I certainly had a deliverer. I had so many manifestations of stress in my body over the last five years that I just could not ignore. I had been going to a friend of mine who did acupuncture. Each visit, the culprit of my ailments was always stress. He would gently ask each visit have you been looking for other jobs? This question made me uneasy because I knew what I needed to do. So like any good fear wearing Christian, I quit going to see him.

If I chose to stay in my current job, I knew that it meant more work, more hours outside of school, and more stress. I was pouring out all day at school emotionally and then I was coming home and pouring myself out emotionally and spiritually. I felt like I had no time to devote to the church. I felt as though I was like one of the Israelites trying to keep up the quota of bricks with less hay. The tension in my spirit was that I knew Jesus wanted to do more with less, not work more to achieve less. He wants to give you more money in less hours. He wants to give you more favor for less striving. I fear that we have relegated rest and relaxation to one week of the year. If rest became our lifestyle, we might think something was wrong.

On April 12, 2021, I made the decision after preaching the day before that I was going to resign. I was waiting for peace to come to guide this decision and it finally came. Josh and I had completed an application to refinance our house a few weeks before that Sunday. We thought lowering our monthly payment could only help if I decided to step away from public education. The next day, I received some emails from our bank that needed to be reviewed and signed for the loan application. When I opened those materials, it showed me exactly how much credit card debt we had, and I was floored. I don't know why I was so shocked, considering that we paid for my Master's Degree and Rank 1 on our own, without taking out student loans. But by not taking out student loans, we incurred debt in other ways. I immediately had this pit in my stomach about my decision. Why couldn't I have seen that statement a week ago? Three days ago? The enemy knew I had just settled the decision in my heart, and wanted to thwart any action on my part to continue. I could have looked at that number and allowed it to stop me and told myself that staying would help us pay off that debt.

Here's the thing- staying in that job for the last ten years never helped us pay off that debt. Call me crazy, naive, stupid, or full of faith- that document only solidified that if this was going to work, it had to be God. If our step of faith was to be a story we would tell our grandchildren, and the next generation, we KNEW that it had to be impossible. On April 16, 2021, I met with my principal and tearfully gave him my letter of resignation. Even in that moment of handing him that letter, I was both sad and alive all at the same time. I knew that I still had a job to do and contract days that needed my full attention. My principal was great about the whole thing, and even prayed with me before I left his office. I knew how hard it was for him to hear this news, but I rejoice that I made a friend that cared more about my destiny than a position. That evening, I came home with mixed emotions. I remember Josh asking me why I was not more excited, and all I could feel was that pit in my stomach. I immediately became aware of the potential risk I was putting my boys into. I was having second thoughts. That night, I had my first ever panic attack. The weight of the decision I had made and thereby made official was heavy. There were moments I could not breathe and I cried for two days. I thought about how guidance counselor positions do not come open very often. I thought about retirement and insurance. I couldn't sleep that night and I remember thinking they were going to post my job immediately and that I could not undo what I had just done. At 12:30 in the morning, I texted a friend of mine who worked at the board office and I told him I may have made a mistake and could I have the weekend to think about my decision. He obviously did not respond right away, so that sent me into an even darker tailspin. I was so gripped by fear and despair, that I was willing to do anything to make that feeling go away.

"When Pharaoh let the people go, God did not lead them on the road through the Philistine country, though that was shorter. For God said, 'if they face war, they might change their minds and return to Egypt.' So God led the people around by the desert road toward the Red Sea" (Exodus 13:17-18 NIV).

I'm so glad the Lord did not take me out of Egypt on the quicker route, because if he had of, I certainly would have turned back. Process is not quick. Me arriving at this point in my life was not quick, and I am not sure why I assumed that a sudden drop off in the promised land would be quick either. Saturday was a little better but not much. I woke up tired from not sleeping and I still had this pit in my stomach that made eating hard to do. Your calling is not realized overnight, and it shouldn't be abandoned overnight either. That evening, Josh and I had a long talk and he firmly reminded me that if I turn back, I am making the decision out of fear. Fear does not originate from God, and in fact, he does not give us a spirit of fear. The enemy wanted me to focus on the what-ifs and God wanted me to start to see the even ifs. Isaiah 41:10 says "Fear not, for I am with you" (NKJV). Jesus is not saying that we will never feel fear. But we should not allow fear to control us and prevent us from moving forward. True courage is moving forward in the face of fear. Psalm 34:4 "I sought the Lord and required of him and he heard me and delivered me from all of my fears" (AMPC). Every decision you make based on fear will not be in accordance with God's will.

We have to keep ever before us that fear paralyzes and faith mobilizes. Even after I made it official that I had resigned and my co-workers were finding out, I had a very hard time visualizing what was next. Faith starts with knowing what it is letting go of, and waits to be astonished at what it will take hold of. There were days I lived on faith scriptures I wrote in my moleskin journal. I would have to close my office door at work and just cry and read those to myself until I had enough courage to keep walking. We want the empty tomb, but we do not want the crucifixion. My weekend was a spiritual red sea. Was I really willing to cross over? I had made the decision to resign and agreed to leave Egypt, but would I take another step and draw a line in my mind and in my heart? I started thinking of my boys again and the "life" I gave them gainfully employed. The Holy Spirit dropped a bomb in my spirit and said either they imitate your fear or they imitate your bravery. What if this one decision changed their destinies? What if they caught the faith it took to take this step and that gave them a staircase to dream for the impossible? If I wanted to continue and not rescind my resignation, I had to cross the red sea with my fears at my heels and allow the Lord to destroy them. I'm sure when the Israelites crossed the red sea and saw what was on the left and the right they may have wondered when is this going to overwhelm me? When is this going to take me out? How long before the waters give way? No one can stay in that place of fear and dread, you have to cross over. The wilderness is where God prepared you for the promise he's given you. It's in the confusing between times that God does some of his best work. God eventually wanted to take the Israelites to the promised land but the destination at first was just to worship. I wonder how many questions turn to doubts when we forgo worship and prayer and just assume? Where you are going is greater than where you've been. We are not called to be slaves to fear, but we are called to be children of God.

Has chaos become so familiar that we are okay with the pain it causes because we know what to expect? Peace and joy are uncharted and terrifying territories, but they shouldn't be. Unbelief never lets us get past the difficulties. Faith does not minimize the dangers and difficulty but looks away from them to God. We can grow so comfortable with fear that we don't know how to live without it. Do you prefer living with the familiar, rather than being freed to experience the unknown? As incredible as it seems, the Israelites were angry at Moses for disrupting the life of slavery to which they had grown accustomed. Have you been lulled into a comfortable relationship with your bondage? Do you fear change more than you fear God? Moses never said I want to go back to Egypt- back to the palace. He had an encounter with God in the wilderness. We need to stop making a case for what's killing us , and start building a case of trust that includes taking a risk. Instead of downplaying uncertainty, we should be welcoming it and kicking comfort and familiarity to the curb. You cannot lead people to a place you have never been, and you cannot lead people to places you are not willing to go. You do not have to know the steps in order to trust. He may not give you all the information upfront. He's likely going to give you bread for the day that you have to go out to gather each morning and quail in the evening.

Knowing the specifics upfront would not be exercising much faith. If we really want to live the life God intends, we have to be willing to let go of the familiar. Let go of the need to control it, fix it, manipulate it, dominate it. The next season will include a guide. Jesus doesn't always drop a map in your lap and program the destination in your GPS. But he does promise to "by day the Lord went ahead of them in a pillar of cloud to guide them on their way and by night in a pillar of fire to give them light, so that they could travel by day or night" (Exodus 13:21-22 NIV).

Jesus might not be asking you to resign from your job, but he may be asking to take a step in faith. Some of us have one foot on the dock and one foot on a boat and that is really unstable. Jesus asked Simon in Luke 5 to put out into deep water and let down his nets for a catch. Simon had been trying to catch fish all night with not much luck. Because Jesus asked him to do it, he agreed. When Simon did what the Lord told him to do, he caught so many fish that he was worried his net might break. Both boats were full of fish from one catch that came from listening to and obeying what the Lord asked him to do. Those men left everything they had to follow Jesus to become fishers of men. It cost them their boat. Those men didn't know that when they left everything, they would GAIN EVERYTHING. From a human or worldly perspective, that might have looked like a dumb decision. Their boats were full of fish. Leaving their boats full of fish meant that someone else would get their provision, and their position. They had been fishing all night and had not caught anything. Some of us have been up all night just trying to make it, striving, and doing what we know how to do. Leaning in and hearing God and doing what he tells you to do changes everything. Jesus changes everything. It's hard to imagine doing something that you have no roadmap for or grid. Jesus is ready to take you off-road and drive for once. I made a decision to stop eating fear and to step out into the deep waters of the unknown.

CHAPTER 10

RELYING ON RAVENS

- AUGUST 2021 -

Obedience is key when we are walking out promises from God. Faith is the substance of things hoped for and the evidence of things unseen (Hebrews 11: 1 NKJV). There will be times when your circumstances do not look like what you thought they would, but that does not change the promise. Obedience has to rest on trust and the truth. You have to trust the truth of his word and the words he has spoken to you. I would like to think we are bubble wrapped in Romans 8:28, and when all else fails, if I truly believe this word- I am safe. The struggle with "all things God works for the good of those who love him" is that most of the time I am the one trying to work and I believe more in me than God. I thought the hardest part about resigning and saying yes to God would have been finances, but this past summer that has not been the issue at all.

I do not think I realized how much of my identity was wrapped up in what I did for a living. More than just a wage, what I did was my status, what I hid behind, what I poured into, and what I was programmed to do for so long. I remember telling Josh that I couldn't just shut down or turn off that kind of routine that drove our life for so long. Our boys are getting ready to go back to school, and honestly it is just weird. I've never had to worry about drop-offs and pick-ups and work that out with Josh before now. There was a pace to my work day and year that had become so second nature to me that when that pace changed, it literally felt like I was not doing enough. I went from being an equal breadwinner to a bread eater and that made me feel some kind of way. I've had a job since I was fifteen and even though I work for our church now, I just felt like I was slacking. I felt this need to not spend any money. I was depressed. I missed being a professional. There was a transition happening with my job but also at our church. I was so sure that one piece would not change and when it started to shift, I was lost. It was evident that I was in a season of resetting. You cannot undo ingrained patterns of behavior in nine weeks' time. The boys will be going back to school soon, and I think I need to give it time. I'm not sure if I miss my old job and my old colleagues or if I miss feeling productive. I miss the structure. The problem with all of this is that I was trusting my feelings more than what God had told me. Feelings belong to us, but they are not supposed to be used as the only guide when making decisions and certainly not when it comes to moving forward. I had forgotten to rejoice. Sometimes we need to call grief out for what it is, feel the feels and then MOVE ON. My problem as a typical four is that I want to cozy up in the vat of feels and stay there. My feelings of fear kept me in the vat for years, and now it was time to rejoice, connect with the father, and move.

ELIJAH AND THE RAVENS

When I think of obedience and living a nomadic lifestyle, I think of Elijah. The voice of God does not say only one thing to us. He does not tell us to do only one thing. Obedience moves with what the Lord has said, and waits to get further instruction. Obedience does not make its own way. In this season, I do not want to pull a Hagar. God told Abraham to leave his country, his family, and his covering to go to a land the Lord would show him (Genesis 12:1). Like Abraham, I know what I have left, but I do not know exactly where I am going. It is not documented in scripture, but I am sure Abraham had his days where he struggled with that. He got impatient with God and had a son with Hagar before he had one with his wife. I encourage you to wait on God. If you are in a season of obedience, just wait. What we do with the time in between what was promised and the manifestation is so important. Our ability to rejoice and be thankful in the unknown is paramount. Grumbling, making our decisions apart from God's leading, and impatience could result in delays. In 1 Kings chapter seventeen, we read about Elijah. Elijah told the king that it was not going to rain for a few years. After that, the Lord told Elijah to leave that place and hide in the Kerith Ravine, where he would drink from the brook and be fed by ravens. Yes, you read that right- the Lord directed ravens to feed Elijah at that place. You are going to be fed at the place God told you to go, nowhere else. Elijah set the example for loyal obedience. He had to trust God for provision when times were bleak. He had to stand firm in faith for God's promises to be fulfilled.

How many of us would be willing to do what Elijah did? How many of us would be willing to accept being fed by ravens? I bet Elijah was tempted to ask God for a different carrier of his food! Ravens are scavengers, and they eat the flesh of dead animals. Even though the popular opinion of ravens now and then was not great, God cares for them too. Jesus provides food for the young ravens when they call (Job 38:41 NIV). Scripture tells us that ravens do not sow or reap, they have no storeroom or barn, and yet God feeds them. And how much more valuable are you than birds! (Luke 12:24 NIV) If being free and walking out your destiny means that you will be fed from the saliva of a raven carrying your bread, would you do it? Talk about a change of pace! Not only can we go grab food or have it delivered at the touch of an app, but we are in the habit of ordering what we want when we want it. Obedience might require going to the spot where you are cut-off from the familiar. The word Kerith means a cutting or a separation. Elijah had to wait to eat. He ate when the ravens brought his food. I wonder how long it took him to be thankful for what they brought?

We sold my car a few months back. The car is about nine years old and it was either put down some serious cash to keep it in good shape, or sell it now for a decent amount. By selling my car, that meant I started driving our Jeep Patriot that is almost 14 years old. I do not like driving that car. I miss my leather heated seats, my bluetooth capabilities and the luxury of that smooth ride the Dodge Journey afforded me. Instead of being a brat, I need to appreciate the Jeep Patriot. I should be thanking God I have a car. According to Graham Cooke, timing is up to God but preparation is up to us. How I steward the in-between matters. Even though he was fed by ravens, Elijah was hidden from his enemies. The Kerith Ravine afforded Elijah a respite, a sanctuary to re-group, re-set, and re-align. Will we follow Jesus and be obedient even when it does not make sense to us? Elijah did not escape the drought. He knew before he left for the Kerith Ravine that there would not be rain in three years. Elijah did what God asked him to do but he still felt the effects of the drought. I have taken the first steps in what God asked me to do, but I am still feeling the effects of that decision. The high school I worked at is a half-mile from my backyard. My oldest son will be there next year and his current school is next door to where I used to work. On the days when I take him to school, I will be reminded of what I walked away from when I resigned. I am sacrificing a little to make this new way of life work. I can't just go out and buy a new car right now. I still see former co-workers in the grocery store. I am not walking in the fullness of fulfillment right this second, but it's coming. Obedience started out feeding one person, but if you read on in Elijah's story, it eventually fed three people. And if you keep going, obedience fed 100 prophets. Your first step of obedience will reap a harvest.

Promises are a beautiful partnership, but they are not always glamorous. The process to get to your promise is not always easy, but it is worth the journey. When I was a teenager, I attended a youth group at my church called The Furnace. Wednesday nights at our church were lit. We were falling out, crying out, and casting out and were there some nights until 10:00 p.m. My youth pastor was obsessed with fire. He began state-wide youth conferences called Firefall. I went to the Brownsville, Florida revival when I was a sophomore in high school, a mission trip my junior year, and by the time I became a senior, I knew what I wanted to do. I wanted to graduate high school and go into full-time ministry. I did not want to take the ACT or apply to college because I was convinced of God's power. I remember telling my mom my plans and she lovingly told me I needed to go to college. The only reason I received the scholarship I did was that not many people applied for it, and it was a full ride. I wanted the high of the conferences all the time, and not the responsibility. I wanted to jump right into ministry and forget the process because I thought I was ready. If God had given me what I thought I wanted, what I thought I was ready for and given me the full plate I was craving, I would have buckled under the pressure and gone back to Egypt. I was not strong enough in my faith at that time to undergo that kind of setback.

Ministry is not a fairy tale, it is not always being swept away to Winds of Worship number 5. Ministry is blood, sweat, and tears.

Ministry is when you have worked all day, come home to power clean dog hair tornadoes quickly off of the floor and make sure there are no pee stains on the guest toilet. The Ministry is counseling a married couple on the brink of divorce until 8:00 p.m., put your kids to bed, have 10 more text messages unread on your phone, and meanwhile you are contemplating the dinner you have yet to eat. The wait time on your process is not a punishment, but a proposed, prescribed time that will lead to promotion. He will not send you to the interview to change your destiny unprepared. The greater the purpose in your life, usually the more protracted the process is. The promise of being in full-time ministry has not been wasted or forgotten. A few Sundays ago, I thought to myself "we eat good at Kingdom House." We went from barely eating spiritually to feeding, and it's not Ramen noodles. Thank you, Lord, that we are eating well in the house. It's not from the mouths of ravens, but from the breath of God. The key to promises is being okay with the process. "Consider it a sheer gift, friends, when tests and challenges come at you from all sides. You know that under pressure, your faith-life is forced in the open and shows its true colors. So don't try to get out of anything prematurely. Let it do its work so you become mature and well-developed, not deficient in any way" (James 1:2 MGS). Your purpose and your process were chosen by God long before you were born.

Randall Worley, in his book Wandering and Wondering, says that "tragically the purpose that is growing inside each one of us is often stillborn- not due to illegitimacy but to premature delivery. We must learn to be patient" (54). God wants to do the impossible through us and with us. If the promises were possible, it would exclude God. We ought to be dreaming so big that it scares us. My dream of leaving my job and being full-time at the church scared me to death for years. I am in my own Kerith Ravine where the Lord is revealing to me where I have put false comfort and security. I have been so upset by walking away from being a professional and wasting the degrees I have. None of these earthly crowns are going to matter when I get to heaven. I am not storing up treasures in heaven clinging to degrees. I am going to love him better because of this process. I am walking out a promise of God as we speak. I look back at those high school years and I am so grateful. I was about to forgo higher education to pursue ministry as a young 17-year-old girl. Now I am giving God the sacrifice of my obedience, and laying down the college and graduate school I went through to be taught and transformed in the presence of Jesus. He does not waste a thing. There would be no hemming without things coming unraveled. For the first time in my life, I know I am right where I need to be. Psalm 139:5 is my favorite verse and the basis for this book. I love how this verse reads in The Passion Translation "You've gone into my future to prepare the way, and in kindness you follow behind me to spare me from the harm of my past." God knows the future, so he knows how to craft our days. He knows our past, so he knows how to accelerate and ordain our steps. Where I am walking is no surprise to him. Where you are walking and about to tread is no surprise to him either.

CHAPTER 11

GET ON WITH IT

Looking longingly out into the sum collection of my life where it stands, my window acts as my periscope and frame. If obedience is measured by leaving everything behind to follow the nudging you haven't been able to shake, then I sit here proud and honored to truly serve the King. I see the trampoline anchored to the back yard, a metaphor for how we are about to launch. I see the fence that Josh built and assembled by hand, each slate of each board strategically placed to secure the borders of our lot. Behind the fence is a trail, and taking it leads to possibility. The full trees give way to a gray sky, where at this very moment is a heavy rain. Taking in this scene for the first time really, a peace that has become very normal lately evades my mind and fills my heart with assurance. I've done something drastic and wild! Walking by faith went from an idea to a reality. I've ventured out, and I am storing up treasure not on this side of heaven where moths can destroy but heaping coals on my head. I stopped talking about leaving, and I left. I willingly build an altar and give God my fears, my family, and my future. This life is not my own. I have resigned my understanding for peace that passes all understanding. We know in part, see in part, and prophesy in part. If we trust the Lord, then we cannot defend our ability to understand. There is a weight exchange when we lean. I'm learning to lean less on my ways and lean more on his higher ways. The letting go has meant an opening up. The safety on my spiritual trigger has been dismantled. The spiritual floors of our house are littered with the casings of faith and hope aimed and TRIED. The oaks of righteousness have been planted and they are growing taller, and I see them out the window. My faith is no longer concealed but out in the open and the dance is spinning and twirling me to the tune of reckless abandon.

I got out of the boat, and I am taking Jesus at his word. I feel free, inspired, and completely sure of the goodness of God. I still contend that I would rather dive in, and have to be rescued by the life preserver of Jesus than to have never felt what getting my garments soaked feels like. All this talk of faith feels like real life and is making me feel alive under the collar. I will keep standing tall knowing in my heart and in my spirit that my view of life where it stands right now is changing, and I am changing.

When we step into new seasons, it's an invitation to be sifted. We cannot take on the change we have either asked for or the change we are currently walking in without our spiritual bodies undergoing change as well. Right now, I am questioning whether or not I can survive the change and the answer to prayer. What I would normally hide behind, use as my martyrdom, and my excuse is gone. Right now, I want to put the professional cloak back on. Right now, I want to put the gainfully employed cloak back on. I knew how to do life with those cloaks on. I knew how to savor the weekends, savor the little time I had off of work, I knew how to wade stress. Right now, I am exposed. Right now, I have nothing to hide behind. Right now, I have a wide-open calendar and instead of that feeling like freedom, it feels suffocating. Right now, all I can do is look at my own soul. Jesus is singeing away pride. He is casting down idols and all the false senses of identity I used to wear. The bible says his power works best in our weakness (2 Corinthians 12:9 NLT). Growth is not always about what feels good. We want the resurrection without the crucifixion. In order for Peter to be the solid rock that the church would be built on, he had to undergo some sifting.

CHAPTER 12

SIFTED AS WHEAT

- OCTOBER 2021 -

Peter is the disciple that gives me hope. He was one of Jesus' closest friends and one of few people to witness the transfiguration. Just because he witnessed Jesus' transfiguration, he still had to undergo one himself. Upon meeting Simon, Jesus changes his name, saying "you shall be called Cephas (which is translated Peter)" (John 1: 42 AMP). Peter was the man God would later use to start the early church, but he was wonderfully human. One minute Peter is getting the keys to the kingdom of heaven, and the next he was cutting a Roman soldier's ear off. Peter's life shows us that we cannot live from previous encounters, no matter how profound. Peter physically walked with Jesus, reclined with him, had coffee and conversation with him, and yet denied him.

"'Simon, Simon, Satan has asked to sift all of you as wheat. But I have prayed for you, Simon, that your faith may not fail. And when you have turned back, strengthen your brothers.'

But he replied, 'Lord, I am ready to go with you to prison and to death.' Jesus answered, 'I tell you, Peter, before the rooster crows today, you will deny three times that you know me.'" (Luke 22:31-34 NIV).

The purpose of sifting wheat is not to destroy it but to remove the chaff– the dust, husks, and impurities. The sifting process is uncomfortable and even painful but it's effective. When we are sifted as wheat, there is an assurance that we will emerge free from impurities. The weaknesses are removed, the failures are shaken away, and we will emerge strong in Jesus. Growth is usually not about what feels good. Being sifted is a work in us to remove what isn't of God, and then we can help strengthen others. Jesus told Peter when you turn back strengthen your brothers. Sifting means multiplication. If wheat was not sifted, it would be compromised. You cannot eat wheat as it is in its initial form. Sifting or threading is done to release the inedible chaff from the usable , edible grain. This process helps to separate that which is good and suitable from that which is useless. Separate that which is good and usable from my baggage, my so-called securities, my false identity, my theology, my opinion, and my feelings. I thought resigning from my job would be the hardest thing I would ever do. Since I made the decision to be more available for ministry, I feel like I have gone through this stripping down season. I feel like I'm being stripped down- the carpet is being pulled back and the original hardwood floors have been exposed. When I look at a piece of wheat, I think to myself I've always looked like this God.

Stepping out in faith will force you to pass every buoy of comfort you knowingly clung to and the ones you never knew you rested and relied on. Our faith has to rest on the solid rock of Jesus Christ and Him alone. Our political positions, our tax bracket, our insurance policies, our retirement funds, the cars we drive, and every other source other than Him has to be laid down.

I'm almost 40 and I don't know how to start over. I've always looked like this piece of wheat- this is what I know. There are parts of my being that have to go, that have to be pruned, that have to be sifted. Like Peter, I thought my life was glorifying Jesus and maybe it was, but to move forward in faith, I can't take what used to work with me. I thought this was one big resigning but this has been so much more. It is a continual lying down, a continual stripping, a continual acknowledgment of false idols, false safety, false security, a misaligned purpose and an identity that will continuously be formed and refined. I'm finding out how much I hid behind my job. I excused certain things because I was always working. I enjoyed certain things because I was always working. Now I'm like a musician that has been asked to come out from behind their instrument and I feel awkward, not sure what to do with my hands, and I am learning how to worship without that. It's been the hardest season but I feel closer to Jesus. I'm learning how to really depend on Him.

We can survive the sifting. "But I have prayed for you, Simon, that your faith may not fail, and when you have turned back, strengthen your brothers. " How I wish Jesus would have said I Prayed for you Simon that this would blow over, and not happen. Jesus already knew Acts 2 and what Peter would do and he needed a real ride or die disciple, one that had endured the cross himself. When Satan sifts believers, his goal is to damage our faith so much that we're useless to God. The enemy wants us shelved far away from the action of the Lord's kingdom. We must suffer with Christ if we would be glorified with him. Through suffering and trial, our faith is refined. God prayed for Peter before he was sifted and He prays for us in our trials and intercedes on our behalf. Even though we walk through the valley of the shadow of death, He is with us. The same Peter who denied God went on to be one of the major players in establishing the church we see in Acts.

"Even though you have to put up with every kind of aggravation in the meantime. Pure gold put in the fire comes out of it proved pure; genuine faith put through this suffering comes out proved genuine. When Jesus wraps this all up, it's your faith, not your gold, that God will have on display as evidence of his victory. You never saw him, yet you love him. You still don't see him, yet you trust him—with laughter and singing. Because you kept on believing, you'll get what you're looking forward to: total salvation. So roll up your sleeves, get your head in the game, be totally ready to receive the gift that's coming when Jesus arrives. Don't lazily slip back into those old grooves of evil, doing just what you feel like doing. You didn't know any better then; you do now. As obedient children, let yourselves be pulled into a way of life shaped by God's life, a life energetic and blazing with holiness. God said, "I am holy; you be holy." You call out to God for help and he helps—he's a good Father that way. But don't forget, he's also a responsible Father, and won't let you get by with sloppy living." (1 Peter 6-17).

The sifting season is not to punish you, but rather to strengthen you. Peter could have stayed someone who just really loved Jesus and who witnessed a lot of really cool miracles. He and Judas both were being sifted as wheat. The difference- Peter realized what he had done and scripture tells us he wept bitterly. But because his faith was tested and he matured, he was able to become a grain of wheat that multiplied the church. If you want to stay in a bubble of a one way relationship just loving God and have some cool experiences you can. Or your faith can be tested and you can be refined in the fire and molded into gold. If wheat stays in its original form it cannot feed anyone. But when it's beaten and broken down to the grain, the grain can turn into flour and flour into bread, and bread into loaves and it can multiply and feed a lot of people. Sometimes we have to let go of something to be used for something else. Sometimes God needs to sift our own confidence and our own faithfulness. He's sifted how I lean on me. He's sifting through how I answer life's problems. He's sifting my reliance on anything but him. The enemy sifts you to destroy you unmercifully. Our father sifts us to get rid of the junk. He's sifting you because he loves you.

My mom always used to say before she would spank me, this hurts me more than it hurts you. I'm doing this because I love you. You are not above discipline, you are not above sifting, you are not sinless. I thought I was ready, I thought since I've been a part of the ministry here at Kingdom House that I was ready to go full-time. I feel like I can identify with Peter. I really do love the Lord but I don't always think my actions point people to him. I wouldn't say I've publicly denied him but I would say I privately have. There have been times that I have been so disappointed in life and I have blamed him for it. Thank goodness Jesus knows my heart and that he sees ahead. He speaks to the person I will be and not the one that's about to break his heart. Peter went from the man who physically experienced Jesus to the broken vessel that lived with the Holy Spirit and was directed by the Holy Spirit. Some of the greatest encouragement and scriptures in the New Testament come from Peter and they come from a place where faith has been tested and been proven. Peter was sifted like wheat and he was reduced to a grain that multiplied the New Testament church. His testimony produced go-to verses that you and I read today to have the strength to take one more step. I remember hearing Bill Johnson say one time that maturity is expensive. He could not be more right.

My fear is that the bride of Christ would rather take a counterfeit destiny than to wade the hard things. I do not know if I am at the place where I consider hard times a gift, but that is where I should be headed. "Consider it a sheer gift, friends, when tests and challenges come at you from all sides. You know that under pressure, your faith-life is forced into the open and shows its true colors. So don't try to get out of anything prematurely. Let it do its work so you become mature and well-developed, not deficient in any way" (James 1:2-4 MSG). If you and I can contend with difficulty, we will stand. If we can take every fear, every so-called security and give it to Jesus and not take it back, man oh man would we be miles ahead. This next year for me will be very interesting. I feel like I have finally come out of the hallway, and now I am in a room. I have to keep ever before me, that I have come a long way to be in this very room. I've paid a high price to be in the room. I might not have all the details, but I have stepped into a room. And now that I am in the room, I am ready for whatever God has for me and I am ready to go where He sends me. I just feel overwhelmingly open. I am open to whatever the Lord wants to do.

I feel like my life has been culminating to this moment for almost six years. The details of my whole life have been stitched and hemmed by the master seamstress. He's the type of seamstress that allows us to pick any clothes and he is faithful to tailor the fit. He's also the type of designer that has a one-of-a-kind suit taken in for our exact fit and measurements, that he has been hoping we would one day want to wear. He's got a dress that curves and accentuates our edges, our frame, our purpose, and our talents. The beautiful thing about our loving father is he will bless us no matter what, but I feel like we all know what we should be doing. He is not the earthly father that cuts us off if we choose a life or a lifestyle that is not in alignment with what he foresaw for us. There is too much at stake and too many people hanging in the balance for Jesus not to use us where we are, and use our lives as a vessel for the presence. However, when the purity of heart to please him and his power collide, spiritual fireworks are exploding in the heavenlies. To know yourself is to know God.

I keep thinking about one of my favorite Disney movies, Sleeping Beauty. There was such a divide over whether Princess Aurora's dress would be pink or blue. Aurora in Latin means "dawn." Jesus has literally brought the dawn to me, a new day. If you are still reading this and haven't fully realized that our Lord and Savior is working all the details out for your good- He is! He won't rush you, but he will gently and subtly nudge you along the road of transformation. He loves us too much to allow us to stay the way we have always been. I should love him so much that I willingly accept that fact and I guard the integrity of my heart. Whatever happens from here, I know it will be amazing because he has my life in the palm of his hand. Every second of every day has been overseen and orchestrated by the Lord, and I do not know why I should ever expect that a minute of any time I have left has not already been ordained for his purposes. The storm is all around, but I've stepped out of the boat and my eyes are locked on the face of the one my heart loves. I am ready to move about in what He has for me, everything and nothing less. Let's get on with it!

WORKS CITED

CHAPTER 8

Campbell, Mike. "Meaning, Origin and History of the Name Jochebed." Behind the Name, *https://www.behindthename.com/name/jochebed.*

CHAPTER 9

Worley, Randall. Wandering and Wondering: The Process That Brings Purpose. Whitaker House, 2017.

CHAPTER 10

Campbell, Mike. "View Message." Behind the Name - the Etymology and History of First Names, *https://www.behindthename.com/bb/fact/1835.*

Worley, Randall. Wandering and Wondering: The Process That Brings Purpose. Whitaker House, 2017.

CHAPTER 12

"Aurora (n.)." Etymology, *https://www.etymonline.com/word/aurora.*

ABOUT THE AUTHOR

Melissa Settles is a wife and mother. Melissa and her husband, Josh Settles, live in Shelbyville, Kentucky. Together they are raising two young men, Connor and Cooper. They are also raising a Golden Retriever named Seger who keeps them all entertained. Together they pastor Kingdom House, a church they planted in 2013. Melissa and her husband carry a deep passion to see the local church mobilized. Josh and Melissa's vision is to expand God's kingdom by releasing freedom, hope, and love. Their heart is to see every believer function in a lifestyle of the supernatural. Melissa is a co-pastor, certified Teacher and Guidance Counselor, and a certified Enneagram Coach. Melissa has always been drawn to writing and journaling, dating back to handwritten prayers as a child and bible study notes as a teenager. Journals upon journals liter her book shelves and are considered one of her prized possessions. To chronicle the journey has been her greatest reward and to see the goodness of the Lord behind and before as He weaves all things together. Where there is transparency, there is freedom. In the chaos, the comforts, disappointments, and joy; her soul is set free when she lets it lead the way on the written page. Thus far, watching the master seamstress HIMSELF at work, has been her biggest honor. For more information about Melissa, you can visit her online:

Website: www.melissasettles.com
Instagram: settles_with_words • **Facebook:** /SettleswithWords

Kingdom House
1857 Midland Blvd. Suite 2, Shelbyville, KY 40065

Made in the USA
Monee, IL
28 February 2022

92025687R00063